THE
ENLIGHTENMENT
Bari Semovski

CONTENTS

THE ENLIGHTENMENT

Enlightenment means to gain deep insight into the meaning and purpose of all things. It means to be able to communicate with, and understand the forces that govern our world. It also means to understand how connected and unified we are with our world. Reaching enlightenment can be a long, difficult process. Some people experience it through trial and error; they live their lives, learn, and get wiser day by day. Others realize that wise people before them have written about their experiences discovering enlightenment; they read these accounts and learn from them. That was my path to enlightenment. I have read and analyzed countless books from subjects ranging from self-help to psychology to spirituality. I've spent hours watching videos of people speaking about enlightenment. I have invested a large portion of my time in conversations about enlightenment, and it has left me with a body of knowledge that can be used to understand the nature of the world we live in. I wouldn't call myself completely enlightened, but I know enough to be able to operate at a higher level, and I know how to teach people to do the same. In writing this book I hope to impart this knowledge to you. I have tested this knowledge against reality as well as against other books and sources of information to ensure congruency.

What I'm going to teach you in this book will change your life. In an ideal situation, you will become enlightened and will be able to connect whole heartedly with the information presented and your belief system will change. In less ideal situations, you will pick up a few things here and there and apply them to your life, or maybe you'll feel motivated enough to finally pursue a career change or perhaps a workout regimen you've been meaning to get to. Either way, one thing this book will not have is no effect. The ideas in this book cannot be read and understood with an open mind and not change at least some aspect of the way you think about the world. It's impossible. These ideas have been collected from several subjects and genres, all of which have already inspired many people; this book simply comprises and connects them. If this is your first self-improvement book, you will be exposed to ideas and techniques that a growing number of people are using to better their lives. If you've read your fair share of self-improvement books, I am sure you will find this book to be a comprehensive road map to enlightenment. You may have heard of these ideas before, but I am confident they have not been presented in such a concise and logical manner as they are in this book. So whether this is your first book or your eleventh, be prepared to be enlightened.

HOLISTIC WORLD SCHEMA

When interacting with the world, our brains cannot process all the information sent our way. There are too many sights, sounds, smells, tastes and textures for our five senses to comprehend. Our brains focus our attention on those things that are most relevant to us in order to avoid an information overload. Our brains do the same kind of focusing when it comes to thinking about the world and storing information related to it. To know how every aspect of the world works in detail would be nearly impossible. Our world is too complex. However, we need to have an understanding of how the world works because our survival depends on it. So what happens is our brains create a mental map for us to follow so we can make quick decisions about people or situations. These maps are called schemas. A schema is a representation in our minds of something in the physical world. For example, most people have a schema of an automobile. When a car is mentioned, their schema of automobiles is primed, causing them to think of things like wheels, engines, doors, steering wheels etc. When a bird is mentioned, their schema for birds is primed, evoking thoughts of beaks, wings, nests and flying.

Schemas are useful to us in that they allow us to store mass amounts of information into one word or phrase. They also give us a shared terminology which makes it possible to have a conversation with someone without having to constantly redefine what we mean by restaurant or computer or tree. The problem with schemas is that they don't leave much room for details. For example, a child who sees someone walking their poodle and is told that it is a type of dog will create the schema of dog, and will think that all four legged creatures with fur are dogs. Next time, when the child sees a cat for example, the dog schema will be primed and they will call the cat a dog. Unless they are corrected, in which case the child will create a new schema to represent cats, the child will continue to mistake cats for dogs. Inconsequential schemas like dogs and cats are easily changed, but when the schema is learned under different circumstances it is not so easily altered. For example, say a child touches a hot stove and gets burned; this child may create a schema to represent stoves that includes the concept of hot, and therefore will not come near a stove again. Telling the child that not all stoves are hot may not be enough to alter their schema. In this case the child may need an experience where they physically touch another stove, learn that not all stoves are hot and remove the concept of hot from their schema of stove. Schemas that affect our survival or are created in emotionally charged situations are more resistant to change.

One of our most important schemas is the one concerning how the world works. This schema tells us how things in the world relate to one another and is essential to our survival. Throughout our lives we have been building on this schema bit by bit and we have developed a way of understanding the world that works for us. You have survived thus far, so your schema, whether it is right or wrong, is able to keep you alive. Your world schema differs from everyone else's because you have had different experiences. Since your schema is different, you behave and interact with the world in a unique way. Although your schema works when it comes to survival, you have to ask yourself, is it the optimal schema to achieve the life you want to live? Your schema was built on life events and knowledge that you may not have wanted to experience or learn, so there is probably unwanted information in your schema that needs to be updated. For example, if you were in a relationship and were abused either emotionally or physically, your relationship schema may lack the concept of trust, which will affect your next relationship. You may think you cannot trust anyone, but that is only because your schema is askew due to the emotional trauma. For another example, people with money and extravagant spending habits may have a shopping schema that includes the concept of buying something based on how much they like it, regardless of the price. However, if they were to encounter tougher economic times and they didn't update their shopping schema to include the concept of frugality, it may lead to financial ruin.

What I propose is that, for the moment, you forgo with your old way of looking at the world and entertain a new outlook for the time being. As good as your world schema may be, there are most likely concepts in there that are holding you back and leading to self-sabotaging behaviors. The schema that I am about to present is not based on my experiences, but rather on research. It is a very general way of looking at the world as to assure its accuracy. Over the years I have tried to disprove this schema, as well as have asked others to disprove it, and all have been unsuccessful at doing so. This schema is a skeleton of the way the world works, and will likely fit into your schema. So keep an open mind as I present to you what I like to call the holistic world schema:

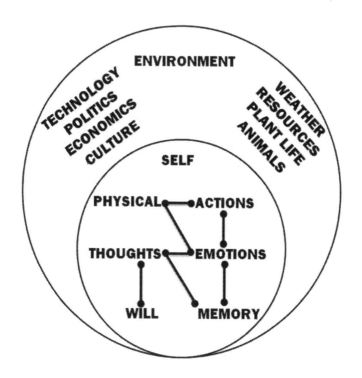

By looking at the diagram you can see the world is divided into two parts - the environment and the self. Within those categories are sub-categories that describe the different aspects of both the environment and the self. Everything in the world can fit into either the environment or the self or one of their subsequent categories. By learning this schema you will have a simplified view of how the world works.

First, we begin with the weather. The weather includes the earth's atmosphere – the ozone layer, the clouds, precipitation, heat, cold, air etc.

Next we move onto earth's resources. This includes the rock that we live on and all its elements – from iron to gold to all of the elements on the periodic table. Resources also include water, other planets and the sun. Other planets represent untapped resources that can be had once we find a way to reach them. Resources include all debris from outer space, however once the debris, let's say a meteorite, enters into the earth's atmosphere, it becomes precipitation and therefore part of the weather category.

There is also a distinction between plant life and resources. Although plant life, like trees for example, are used as resources, the difference lies in the fact that plant life is alive while resources remain inanimate. Plant life includes grass, flowers, bushes, wheat plants, algae, fungus etc.

Our next category is animals. Animals include all four legged creatures, fish, birds, monkeys and human beings – the self is part of the animal category which we will get into shortly. Animals are an important category because human beings have created the next four categories.

Technology is the first of our human-made categories. Technology includes anything that has been made to make our lives easier. It includes inventions like computers and cars, infrastructure like housing and sky scrapers and also things like pens and even cutlery. In the early days, the advancement of technology began with spears and evolved into the more efficient bow and arrow which allowed for more effective hunting. The tribes with the most advanced weaponry were able to gather more food, grow bigger and become more powerful than tribes using less advanced weaponry. Today, technology has brought us such things as guns, tasers, A-bombs and tanks.

When the Europeans discovered the New West, they were able to overtake the natives because their weaponry was far superior. While the natives were using bow and arrows, the Europeans had guns. Whoever has the greater technology has the power. Politics is the category that deals with who has power over whom. Politics includes our laws and the police force and military who enforce them. Although politicians are part of the animal category, the bills they pass are part of the politics category. A stop sign is part of the technology category, but what it represents and how it gets you to stop your vehicle is part of the politics category. Politics includes the judicial system, the concept of a lawyer, fines, laws, political campaigns, elections etc.

Economics includes our economy – our money, the free market, business licenses, stocks and other financial instruments, the job market etc. In the early days, economics was closely tied to food. Whichever tribe had the most food was the wealthiest. Today the wealthiest is the one with the most money. Keep in mind that money is not the paper it is printed on - that belongs to the technology category - but rather, money is the value that is represented by that piece of paper. A one hundred dollar bill is only part of the economics category if other people recognize and honour its value, and are willing to exchange goods and services for it.

Our final category in the environment is culture. Culture is a vast category. It includes the arts, all forms of knowledge – from what's being taught in schools to what's being taught through religion – fashion, the news, live theatre etc. There are some distinctions that must be made with this category, mainly the difference between technology and culture. Music is culture but the iPod the music is stored on is technology. A certain style of clothing is culture, but the clothes themselves are technology.

From there we move onto the self. The self is actually part of the animals category but is separated to allow us to explore it further. The self is made up of six subcategories, the most obvious being the physical. The physical category includes our physical bodies, from our legs to our internal organs. Our bodies are part of the physical category, but the clothes we choose to wear are part of the actions category.

Actions include everything we say and do, including our facial expressions and other non-verbal communications. As you can see in the diagram, the physical category is directly connected to our actions. Any two connected categories influence one another mutually. For example, if we feel sick, we may perform the action of lying in bed all day. On the flipside, if we perform an action that leads us to trip and fall, our physical bodies may be affected by bruising or other injuries.

Our actions are also connected to our emotions. Emotions are the feelings we have that color our experience. We are almost always feeling an emotion, and these feelings effect how we behave. For example, if we are fearful we may perform the action of fleeing a certain situation, whereas if we are feeling happy we may engage in a smile. Emotions are also directly connected to our physical bodies. When we are angry we can feel our blood pressure rising and our muscles tensing. The category of emotions is connected to almost all of the other categories, which speaks to its importance in our lives. Emotions are further connected to our thoughts and our memories.

The category of thought consists of all the things we think of – from images we visualize to thoughts that just pop out of nowhere. Thoughts are separate from our emotions; when we think about someone we love and all the good times we've spent with them, those are thoughts. However the feeling we get i.e. the butterflies in our stomach, increased heart rate etc. is part of the emotions category. Thoughts are connected to emotions in that by what we think, we can change the way we feel and vice versa. Think sad thoughts and you will begin to feel sad. If you are feeling happy, you will think happy thoughts. The category of thoughts is also connected to the category of memory.

Memory refers to our ability to store ideas and images for later retrieval. All our schemas are stored in our memory. Things that we do not wish to remember, like bad experiences, are stored in our memory. Memory is strongly connected to thoughts and emotions. When something happens to us that triggers a similar memory, we begin to have thoughts of that occurrence and start to feel the same feelings we had at that time. If we think about something that made us happy in the past, that memory will be triggered and will make us feel similar to how we felt in that moment.

Whereas the category of emotions is like a hub that connects to five out of six categories, the category of will is only connected to thoughts. Will is our ability to override our natural thoughts. Will is our power to change what we believe, how we feel and our actions. By using our will we can change our thoughts, which then changes how we feel, which then can change our actions. Although will is only connected to one category, it is just as important as emotions.

Now that you are familiar with the categories, let's take a look at how this diagram relates to your life. As mentioned previously, you are represented by the self, and everything else in the world is represented by the environment. Using the example of getting a traffic ticket, let's go through a situation to see how it all ties together. Let's say on a rainy day (weather) you're driving your car (technology) and you exceed the speed limit (politics). An officer (animal) sounds his siren and you see and hear (physical) the lights and the high pitched squeal and pull over (action) to the side of the road.

While waiting for the officer to approach your vehicle you remember the last time you were pulled over (memory) and what a setback it was financially (thought). You begin to get worried (emotion) about the consequences, but tell yourself "everything is going to be all right" (will). You begin to relax (emotion) and your body becomes less tense (physical) just in time to deal with the officer in a calm manner (action). At the end of the interaction you are written a ticket, which you end up paying (economics).

Let's try another example where you go to the movie theatre with your significant other and her dog (animals). You purchase (economics) tickets to a 3D (technology) movie (culture). You watch (physical) the movie and feel entertained and excited (emotion). After the movie, as you leave the theatre you recall (memory) particular scenes in the movie and discuss (action) your take on them (thoughts). A couple days later you remember (memory) how much you liked the music in the movie (thoughts) and begin to feel the excitement (emotion) you felt after watching the movie. You log onto iTunes (technology) and purchase (economics) the soundtrack to the movie (culture). As you listen (physical) to the music, you are reminded (memory) of scenes in the movie (thoughts) that you enjoyed and are feeling happy (emotion) about your purchase. Then you realize that you have to get ready to see your significant other (animal) so you say to yourself "that's enough listening to music, I have to get ready" (will).

As you can see, the diagram does represent your life as well as everyone else's. I encourage you to think of something in the physical world that does not fit into one of these categories. Let me know if you find anything. The reason I encourage you to disprove this diagram is because for one, I am confident that this diagram is an accurate representation of the world and two, in order to go onto the next chapter you are going to need to believe that this diagram or schema does indeed represent the world and how it operates. I already believe wholeheartedly that this schema is correct; I need you to believe also. So go out into the real world and test it for yourself.

POINTS OF INTERACTION

Now that you have accepted the holistic world schema as true, we can begin to delve into more detail about how the environment and the self interact. Take a look at the diagram on the following page.

This version of the diagram shows two of the points of interaction between the self and the environment. We interact with the environment through our physical bodies and our actions. Simply by our physical bodies being in the environment, they are interacting with it. For example, without saying or doing anything, our

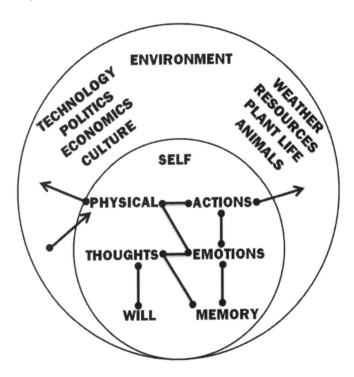

physical bodies are interacting with the environment because other animals are able to see us and think thoughts about us. When it is cold outside we shiver; when it's hot, we sweat. If someone were to accidently hit us with their car, we would be interacting with another animal and technology. Advances in medicine allow for our bodies to heal faster. The environment is constantly interacting with our physical bodies.

The interaction of our actions with the environment is of greater consequence. As stated before, actions refer to everything we say or do, so this is a vast category. Every time we breathe in air, which is automatic, we are interacting with the environment. When we breathe out carbon dioxide, which is also automatic, we are once again interacting with the environment. If we were to stub our toe by accidentally walking into a table, we would be interacting with technology. When we drink water we are ingesting a resource of the environment. If you eat steak and salad you would be eating the environment's plant life and an animal. When we drive a motor vehicle we are emitting pollutants into the atmosphere, thus affecting the weather category. Choosing the clothes we wear influences the category of culture. Through these simple actions alone we interact with the environment, but our actions are far more complex.

Through our actions we can change the environment. For example, if you started your own business selling a new kind of frying pan that changed the way people prepared their meals, you would be changing the categories of culture and economics. If you got into a dispute with someone that led to a physical altercation where the police were involved, your actions would create a reaction in other animals as well as in the category of politics. In summary, our actions lead to a change in the environment, which in turn may affect our physical body in some way. Even if it's as simple as us performing a kind action and a person saying "thank you". That thank you is being heard by our ears, which is part of our physical bodies.

The interaction of our bodies and our actions with the environment is admittedly obvious. What's not so obvious is that there is actually a third point of interaction; our emotions:

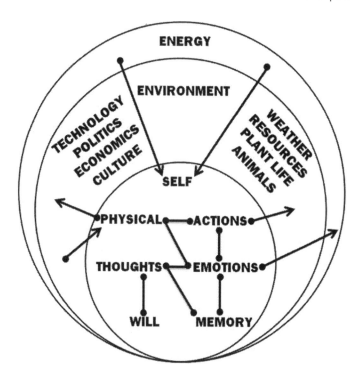

In this version of the diagram we see that there is a whole new category which encompasses the environment and the self. The environment and the self are actually made up of the same thing – energy. In the scientific community it is believed that everything is made up of one basic unit of matter – the atom. If you have a powerful enough microscope you can zoom into any object, such as a chair, a computer or a human, and see that it is made of atoms. If the microscope were powerful enough to zoom in further you would see that atoms are made up of pure energy. This means that everything in the environment, including the self, is made up of the same substance – energy. This energy takes on different forms to create what we see as our world. Energy manifested in a certain way creates a house, while energy manifested in another way creates a dog. Everything is energy, so if we are to learn to operate optimally in our environment, we need to learn to work with energy.

Energy operates on a basic principle called the law of attraction. This law states that like energies are attracted; positive energy attracts other positive energy and negative energy attracts other negative energy. Positive energy cannot come into contact with negative energy because they repel each other. All objects in the environment are set in their levels of positive and negative energy, except for animals. Animals, including the self, are able to shift between positive and negative energies through their emotions. This emotional energy is transmitted into the environment making animals a kind of energy transmitter, and making emotions the third point of interaction in our holistic world schema. When we feel a positive emotion, that energy is transmitted into the environment and because of the law of attraction, positive energy is attracted back to us. When we feel a negative emotion, negative energy is transmitted into the environment and negative energy is attracted back to us.

As I stated earlier, energy takes on different forms to make up all the different objects in our world. The energy that is transmitted from our emotions works the same way. Going back to the diagram, we see that thoughts are connected to emotions. The form our energy takes is determined by our thoughts. When we think a thought, it makes us feel a certain way – either positive or negative – and through that feeling the energy is put out into the environment and returned back to us in whatever form we we're thinking of. For example, if we think about a loved one and that causes us to feel good, that emotional energy will be put out into the environment and will be returned to us in the form of either seeing that person, receiving a call from that person or at the very least having another positive thought about that person. If we think about success and for some reason the thought of success causes us to feel anxious, that anxiety will be put out into the environment and returned to us in the form of opportunities to achieve that unwanted success, or at least ideas on how to achieve that anxiety-inducing success.

With that being said, it is easy to see how our thoughts can attract reality. However, our thoughts are connected to our memory. That's why the past seems to always repeat itself. Here is an example: something happens in our past and is stored in our memory. Whenever that memory is retrieved it brings to mind all the thoughts and emotions associated with that memory. That emotional energy is transmitted into the environment and brought back to us in the form of a similar experience that caused us to store that memory in the first place. Although this happens to a lot of us, we are not helpless when it comes to our memory and reliving our past. Our thoughts are also connected to our will. Using our will we can change any thought we have and replace it with a thought that produces a more positive emotion. When dealing with our past, it is a battle between our will and our memory for control over our thoughts and emotions.

All this talk about the law of attraction and our thoughts being able to attract our reality via our emotions may lead some to believe either, that we are doomed to live a life created by our negative thoughts or that we can sit back and succeed in life through our thoughts. Both of these beliefs are incorrect. Out of the three points of interaction, emotion is the weakest way to interact with the environment. Our physical bodies are of medium strength and our actions are the strongest way to change or influence the environment. Your emotions and energy may bring you opportunities, but without action, your thoughts will not manifest the way you expect them to. Taking action is still the way to achieve your dreams or change your environment. The only difference is now you know that your emotions can make your actions that much more effective.

Knowing the law of attraction, our objective becomes clear – we must think positively in order to attract a better life to ourselves. We must use our will to minimize our negative thoughts and to implant and maximize our positive thoughts. In doing so we will feel more positive, which leads to us transmitting more positive energy, which will be returned to us in the form of positive people, events and circumstances. Your will is the key to accomplishing this. Develop your will and you will be able to leverage the law of attraction to its fullest potential.

As we conclude this chapter, it is time to ask yourself if this makes sense to you. Is the world affected by the way you feel? Can your thoughts really attract reality? Time to put the book down and test it out. Go out into the real world and keep track of what you're thinking and the way you feel and see if your experiences coincide. When you can honestly say that you believe in the law of attraction – and the holistic world schema in general – come back and read the next chapter.

MOMENT TO MOMENT EXPERIENCE

Now that you have accepted the holistic world schema and the law of attraction as fact, we can move into even more detail about how this applies to the moments in your everyday life. If you are having any doubts about the accuracy of either of the concepts, I suggest you take some time and let your own experience prove it to you.

When I speak about moment to moment experience, I am referring to the moments that pass us by and create what we call life. Taken down to its essence, life is nothing more than a series of interrelated moments strung together for us to experience. Some of the moments we experience on our own, some are shared with others. At the end of the day, all we are left with is the memories and the results of our behavior in each of these moments. A moment can be seconds or minutes long; there is no standard length of time that a moment lasts, but we are able to distinguish when one moment ends and another begins. One thing every moment shares is that there is at least one interaction between the self and the environment.

Only one of two possible things can happen in a moment – either we are affecting the environment or the environment is affecting us. In other words, in each moment we are becoming a product of our environment, or our environment is becoming a product of us. In each moment we have a choice: we can either be reactive to our environment, or we can be proactive towards our environment.

The more proactive we are, the more we can change our environment to our liking. If we are always reacting to our environment, we can change very little. For example, say we are driving and someone cuts us off. If we react to their behavior and get angry, we are being pulled into a situation that we have not created, and therefore are less prepared to deal with it. If we react by retaliating and cutting them off in return, we have just entered a new situation not created by our own will. If instead of retaliating, we take a deep breath and take a moment to think about what we want to do next, we will enter into a situation that we created and thus will be better able to deal with it. Who knows, after thinking about it we may let the aggressive driver go and forget about the whole thing. On the other hand, after contemplation we may decide to retaliate anyway – but this time we will be better prepared to return the aggression.

As mentioned earlier, the struggle to put out positive energy into the environment usually comes down to a battle between our memory and our will. Our memory influences our thoughts and emotions to regress to the same way of thinking and feeling that we had in the past. Our will on the other hand injects the thoughts that we want to have, which in turn makes us feel the way we want to feel. If we are weak willed or if our memories are too strong, the past will repeat itself and we will put out the same energy, thus attracting more of what has happened to us in the past. This struggle between our memories and our will has many parallels to the struggle between behaving proactively and reactively; our will being analogous to behaving proactively and our memory being analogous to behaving reactively. If we let our memory win, our thoughts and emotions from the past will be so strong that we will react to our environment. If we exercise our will and think the thoughts we

want to think, we have a chance of sway-
ing our emotions and behaving proactively, thus putting out the energy we want to
transmit and affecting the environment to
our liking.

What this all comes down to is
meeting each new moment with a proactive attitude - specifically an attitude that
lets us experience the new moment and
behave accordingly as opposed to reacting to old thoughts and emotions. But in
order to behave more proactively it will
help to take a closer look at the moments
that pass us by. The following diagram is
a general break down of a moment. (See
flowchart on following page).

As you can see in the diagram, every moment begins with an interaction between the self and the environment. It can
be anything from receiving a phone call
to making a purchase. This interaction
leads to thoughts and emotions flooding
our minds. Depending on the interaction,
these thoughts and emotions can either
be positive or negative. Once we begin

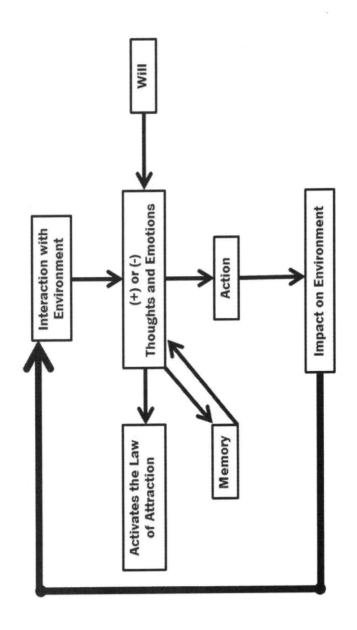

thinking and feeling, three things happen: first, we activate the law of attraction and send out energy into the environment; second, our memory begins to store our current experience; and third, our memory brings up similar past experiences and makes us think and feel how we did at that time. At this time our will comes into play. If we choose to, we can control the thoughts we're thinking and change the way we feel, which will affect the way we're activating the law of attraction and the memories that are being stored. Next, we take some kind of action. This can range from dealing with a situation proactively to reacting to the situation, with doing nothing about the situation lying in between the two. Whatever we choose to do will have some kind of an impact on the environment and that impact leads to the cycle beginning all over again.

Let's use an example to make this clearer. For the initial interaction let's assume our friend has accused us of misplacing their laptop. The interaction would be our friends voice (in the environment) entering our ears (our physical body). From there we begin to think "I am being accused of something I didn't do, this isn't fair" and we begin to feel angry. This negative anger is being transmitted into the environment via the law of attraction and the experience of our friend accusing us is being stored in our memory. Meanwhile, our memory is recalling another time when we were a kid and were accused of taking something that was not ours and got in trouble for it. We begin to feel a sense of fear that this might happen to us again. Our anger and fear is so strong that we immediately take action by refuting their accusation and denying we misplaced their laptop. The impact this has on the environment is making our friend, who believes we are lying to them to cover up, angry. Their anger leads to them telling us they know we are lying and to admit to misplacing the laptop. This accusation of lying is a new interaction with the environment, thus starting the cycle all over again.

In that example we failed to use our will. After our interaction with the environment (being accused of misplacing the laptop) our thoughts and emotions (angry for being wrongly accused and fearing we may get into trouble as we did in the past) were so strong that we reacted and took action right away, instead of using our will to change our thoughts. If we had used our will the situation may have turned out differently. Let's go back in the example to our initial feelings of anger and worry: here we are being accused of something we did not do, but instead of vehemently denying it, we use our will to proactively inject the thought "let me hear him out, maybe there's a good reason he thinks I'm the one who misplaced the laptop". From there our emotions of anger and worry calm down and we do not take any action at all (which is another action all on its own). Our inaction produces a very different kind of impact on the environment; whereas previously our friend became irate, this time our friend calms down. Instead of accusing us of lying, this time he explains why he believes we misplaced the laptop. This explanation is a new interaction with the environment, thus starting the cycle all over again. After hearing our friend's explanation, we think "I should prove that I'm not the one who took the laptop" and take appropriate action to do so. This action impacts the environment by making our friend realize he was mistaken in accusing us and hopefully our next interaction with the environment will be experiencing our friend apologizing to us.

This diagram illustrates exactly what happens in any given moment. In every moment there is an interaction, thoughts and emotions, the activation of the law of attraction, memories being stored and retrieved, the potential for the proactive use of our will and action being taken that impacts the environment. These moments take place back to back and make up the experience we call life. Knowing this, as you experience your life, you will be able to make sense of the moments that pass you by. With the holistic world schema, your schema of the world and how it operates is renewed and updated. With this diagram, you now have a schema for how any given moment unfolds. Going about your day armed with this knowledge will allow you to experience life with a greater understanding than you had before, however, living through the moments with a greater awareness can only do so much to permanently improve your life's circumstances. To truly improve your life, you are going to have to learn how to capitalize on life's moments. The rest of this book will be about instilling in you techniques to be able to do that.

PROACTIVE POSITIVITY

So far you have learned that your emotions give off energy, which is attracted back to you through the law of attraction. Because of this, it is in our best interest to remain positive so we can attract positive people, events and circumstances back to us. You have also learned that there are two kinds of interactions with the environment: proactive and reactive. If we react to the environment it makes it more difficult to change our circumstances. Therefore it is better to be proactive and change our environment to our liking. Put these two concepts together and one can only come to the conclusion that the best way to be is pro-actively positive, meaning we take action to ensure that we remain in a positive state as much as possible. With proactive positivity as our goal, our emotions become of upmost importance. It is our emotions that determine what kind of energy we put out and that determines what kind of energy is attracted back to us. Knowing about the different emotions and how to work with them is the first step in practicing proactive positivity. If we are able to change our emotions at will, not only will we be able to transmit and attract positive energy, but we will also feel better and be in a better mood more of the time.

Emotions consist of a physical arousal in our bodies coupled with a mental label we place on that arousal based on what's going on in the environment. For example, when aroused, our muscles tense up and our blood pressurizes. If something is going on in the environment that is upsetting us, we will label this arousal as anger. If something in the environment is exciting us, we may label the arousal as happiness. This labeling is automatic and happens very quickly. Once we have labeled our arousal, we are moved to behave accordingly. If we are fearful we may try to flee the situation; if we are sad we cry; if we're happy we smile.

Psychological research has shown that there is a set of basic emotions. Psychologists went to different parts of the world, including remote tribes who have little to no influence from the media, and showed them pictures of people making the facial expressions of these basic emotions. In all the places they travelled, people were able to consistently detect the basic emotions correctly. Other emotions like love and hope are universally known and described similarly by people. Although there is no single definitive way to classify emotions, for our purposes, we will use the emotions in the chart on the following page to facilitate our discussion. (See chart on following page).

These emotions can be blended in a multitude of ways to create the hundreds of emotions we can possibly feel. For example, jealousy is a blend of anger and fear. Friendliness is a mixture of happiness and love. Knowing these basic emotions, we can make sense of our emotional life. Another thing to note about the diagram is that the emotions are opposites. Love is the opposite of anger, happiness is the opposite of sadness and faith is the opposite of fear. When you are feeling one of these emotions, it is impossible to feel the opposite. Also, once you feel a positive or negative emotion, feeling similar emotions is more likely. For example, if you are feeling sad, you're one step away from being angry, but miles away from being happy.

Our goal in this chapter is proactive positivity. To achieve that goal we are going to have to learn to minimize negative emotion and maximize positive emotion.

BASIC EMOTIONS

POSITIVE	NEGATIVE
Love A feeling of closeness and extreme liking towards another person or object. Used to facilitate cooperation.	**Anger** A feeling of separation and/or extreme hatred. Used to fight enemies.
Happiness Feelings ranging from contentment to ecstasy. Used to inhibit negativity, promote relaxation and foster enthusiasm.	**Sadness** Feelings of melancholy and sorrow. Used to adjust to a significant loss.
Faith Also known as hope, consists of a feeling that better times are ahead and a higher power is at work in our lives. Used to promote optimism and helps in achieving difficult goals.	**Fear** Feelings of anxiety and worry. Used to flee dangerous situations.

Since life seems to most of us to be a harsh, cruel experience with glimpses of positivity here and there, it would benefit us more to learn how to take our negative emotions and convert them into something useful and positive.

Converting a negative emotion into a positive one is all about exercising your will to change your thoughts. This process is also about timing. We must have the will power to go through the process while we are in the midst of the negative emotion. While you are angry, sad or fearful you must be able to use your will to change your thoughts which changes your emotion. Sometimes this is as simple as forcing yourself to think positive thoughts. If you are in a fearful state for example, you can simply repeat to yourself "I'm not afraid, I'm not afraid, everything is going be okay". Sometimes this works and you're able to talk yourself out of a negative mood.

Another technique you can try is changing your facial expression. Research has shown that when people hold a facial expression that corresponds to a specific emotion, they begin to feel that emotion. For example, if someone holds a smile, they will begin to feel happier and if they frown, sadness sets in. In a study, participants were asked to hold a pencil between their teeth which activated the same facial muscles needed to smile. After doing this for some time, subjects reported feeling happier than before.

A more permanent way we can change our negative moods is by re-encoding our memories. When a memory is retrieved, it is re-encoded with salient information from the present. For example, if you were to think of an incident that angers you, and while thinking of this incident you come to a new understanding of the situation, your memory will be re-encoded in such a way that incorporates this new understanding. Next time the memory is retrieved it will not upset you as much. Re-encoding can be done deliberately, but it will work automatically over time; it's the reason we are able to get over upsets and move on.

These tactics are useful and will get you through mild negative moods. Sometimes however, our negative emotions are so strong that there is nothing you can say or do to get over it. In these cases the simple techniques mentioned above have a minimal effect. For these kinds of situations the process on the following page will be helpful. (See chart on following page).

The first step is to recognize your negative emotions and neutralize it. First you must know your physical symptoms and accompanying thoughts for each of the emotions. For example, when you are sad you feel drained and have depressing thoughts, or when you're worried you feel anxious and think about worst case scenarios. Everybody is different so it's up to you to learn to recognize your own thought patterns and bodily sensations. The other part of this step is neutralizing your emotion. Different things can be

CONVERTING NEGATIVE EMOTIONS INTO POSITIVE EMOTIONS

Recognize and neutralize your negative emotion	Notice your physical symptoms and your accompanying thoughts. Take time to separate your thoughts from your emotions from the situation.
Validate yourself	Recognize that at that point in time, with your frame of reference, you were right to feel the way you felt and behave the way you did.
Identify your unmet need and take action to meet it	Look at how you feel and discern what need of yours is not being met. Decide how you will meet this need and take action to do so.
Explore the other person's frame of reference and forgive them (optional)	See things from their perspective. Once you see where they were coming from and when the thought of the incident no longer upsets you, let them know they are forgiven and wish them well.

done to accomplish this like physical exercise, deep diaphragmatic breathing and any other activity that calms you or makes you happy. If you cannot think of an activity, or are having trouble focusing because you are so upset there are some other methods you can try that work well. Specifically with anger, you can write a poison pen letter which is a letter directed at the person you're angry with, telling them exactly how you feel. These letters usually contain unpleasant, abusive, malicious statements and therefore should probably not be sent to the person. However, the simple act of writing one can neutralize your anger. Another technique you can try and one that I recommend is separating your thoughts from your emotions and the situation. When you go through and separate the situation from your thoughts from how you feel, you are giving your mind a chance to sort out the incident. This leads you to discover things you missed in the heat of the moment and gives you new insight into what really happened.

The next step in the process is to validate yourself. After a dispute with someone, we sometimes see the other person's point of view and blame ourselves for feeling and behaving the way we did. Looking at the other person's point of view too early can lead to us not dealing with our own emotions. Blaming ourselves for negative experiences is counter-productive. Validating oneself is about giving permission to ourselves to behave in ways that are not always perfect, or in other words, to be human. To validate ourselves does not mean to excuse our behavior; it means to recognize that at that point in time, with our frame of reference, we were right to feel the way we did and as a result behave the way we did. Validating yourself can be liberating and give you a feeling of self-acceptance because you are accepting a part of yourself that may not be the best, which is one step closer to accepting yourself as a whole. The mistake people make with validation is that they try to seek it outside of themselves. Sometimes this works. Sometimes you go to a friend or a relative and they take your side and support your behavior, while other times they don't. They may tell you you're wrong and that you need to apologize, which might very well be the case; however, our goal is not to deal with the situation just yet. Our goal is to convert this negative energy into positive energy. So rectifying the situation, which will be necessary later on, is not the best action to take this early in the process.

Once you have validated yourself the next step is to identify your unmet need. Unmet needs are the reason why we feel any negative emotion at all. Looking at the emotion you are feeling and the thoughts that are accompanying that emotion, you can usually discern what need is not being met. Perhaps you're fearful for your safety i.e. maybe someone has threatened to hurt you, or you have a long drive ahead of you in atrocious weather. Perhaps you're sad because you feel like an outsider amongst your friends. Perhaps you've changed throughout the years, but your friends seem to have stayed the same. Perhaps you're angry because someone has disrespected you – maybe they have insulted you in some way or have not given you your three feet of personal space. Whatever your unmet need is, it must be identified and met. The second part of this step is taking action to meet your need. This isn't going to be simple. We cannot control the actions of others, so trying to meet a need - like the need for safety or the need for belonging - by yourself is difficult. How can you belong to a group on your own? If people disrespect you, how can you meet your need for respect? You never asked anybody to disrespect you, that's just how they treated you. This part of the process is challenging and may take a considerable amount of time to accomplish. The important thing is to identify your unmet need and be sure to take action towards meeting it every day. The way you meet your need is up to you. For example, if you have a strong need for safety, maybe you can work on not having to be so certain that everything will be okay. If you have a strong need for belonging, maybe you can work on finding a new social group that is better suited to you. If you have a strong need for respect, maybe you can work on allowing more things to slide, for example if someone bumps into you, you can assure yourself no ill will was meant by it because accidents happen. I'm not saying to let everything slide but just enough so you refrain from entering negative moods as a result of other people's behavior.

By this point in the process you should be feeling a lot better and you should have an action plan for how you will meet your needs and avoid feeling these negative emotions in the future. With that, you will have accomplished your goal of turning your negative energy into something positive and useful. This next step I'm going to mention is optional and only applies if there is another party involved. The final step is to explore the other person's frame of reference and forgive them. At this point it is now time to rectify the situation. Put yourself in their shoes and notice their thoughts and feelings. Try to see where they're coming from. Be careful not to do this too early. Take this step only after you have completed the first two steps and have begun to take action towards meeting your needs. You want to make sure that making amends with this person does not distract from your own feelings. Once you see things from their perspective and can see where they were coming from, and also when you can think about the incident without feeling any negative emotion, let them know they are forgiven and wish them well in the future. Once again this step is optional, but completing it will put forth even more positive energy. The only thing is that it must be genuine. You cannot simply say you forgive the person just for the sake of being proactively positive, you have to mean it and feel it.

Knowing how to convert negative emotions into positive emotions is useful, but let's take it one step further. In order to be able to maximize the positive energy we put out, we need to learn how to enter into a positive emotion at will. Just like we have a procedure to convert negative emotions into positive emotions, we need a procedure to enter into positive states any time we choose. If we only wait for negative moods to be turned positive, or if we are content with our neutral moods, we will be selling ourselves short when it comes to the amount of positive energy we put out. To maximize our positive energy output, we are going to learn to utilize the three positive basic emotions – faith, happiness and love.

Faith, or hope, is the feeling that better times are ahead. It is also the belief that a higher power is at work in our lives and the world is governed by a master plan as opposed to random chance. Faith deals with beliefs, so instead of giving you a procedure you can follow, I can only offer suggestions you can try. If you've read this far and have accepted the law of attraction as fact, you have some faith already. In order to believe the law of attraction is real, you need to accept that the world is not a sequence of random events, and is actually a meaningful string of interconnected moments governed by a higher force (energy). Since you already believe that, you already have a storehouse of faith you can draw upon. Be sure to finish this book and read other spiritual texts; by doing so you will trigger the feeling of faith within you. Something else you can try that will allow you to trigger the milder form of faith – hope – is to visualize what your life will be like when you have it exactly the way you want it to be. The more detailed your visualization, the more engrossing the experience will be. First, don't visualize still images; visualize moving clips of your new life. Don't just watch the clips, interact with them. Visualize in first person and in third person. Visualize in color. Visualize small details; notice how you behave as this new person. Visualize big. If you're picturing a new car, make the car oversized and take in all the details. As you are able to keep your attention focused on your visualization you will begin to feel the sense that all this is possible – that's hope. Another technique you can try is reciting affirmations about your beliefs. Affirm that you believe in the law of attraction and that you are attracting positive energies to you. Remind yourself of your beliefs and faith will begin to rise inside of you.

Whereas faith depends on your beliefs, happiness and love can be triggered with a procedure – by doing certain things, you can elicit these feelings inside of you. There is a large body of research on what makes humans happy. Researchers have conducted experiments where they give people pagers that go off at random intervals. Every time the pager goes off, subjects were instructed to fill out a journal and record what they were doing and how happy they rated themselves to be. Their findings suggest that people are happiest when they are involved in activities that are pleasurable, meaningful and engage them fully. If an activity has these three characteristics, we will be happy doing them. When an activity is pleasurable, we enjoy doing it. That's common sense, but what's not common sense is that participating only in pleasurable activities will not make us happy. You may think that you can be happy if you lay on a beach, play video games or watch T.V all day long, but that is not the case. Sure we will enjoy and extract pleasure from doing these activities, but once we stop doing them, our happiness ceases as well. The reason is that not all pleasurable activities are meaningful. Living for the moment does not make one happy, living in the moment for the future does.

The activities that make people happiest are pleasurable and meaningful to the person's life. Unfortunately most of the activities we are required to engage in are not meaningful, which is why it helps to ascribe our own meaning to them. For example, a brick layer that enjoys his work but is focused on his next break and his paycheck at the end of the week is just doing his job. But a brick layer who thinks about the family that will be moving into the house and how his work is beautifying the community is ascribing meaning to his work. Both brick layers extract pleasure from their job, but the second brick layer will go home feeling happy, while the first brick layer will have to engage in another activity to keep himself happy.

Although pleasure and meaning make an activity worth doing, there is one more criteria for producing long term happiness – optimal experience. Optimal experience or flow, as it's called in the psychology world, is when we are totally engaged in what we are doing. It is that feeling when everything else in the world ceases to exist and all our focus is on what we're doing. You have most likely experienced flow at some point in your life, but just didn't know what to call it. If an activity is pleasurable and meaningful but does not keep you fully engrossed, it will not produce long term happiness. Going back to the brick layer who ascribed meaning to his work, although he enjoys his job and thinks it's meaningful, if he is not in the flow while working, he will not be happy once the day is done. If he does his work and his mind is wandering, happiness will elude him. Pleasure, meaning and flow are the trifecta of happiness.

Love is a feeling of extreme liking towards a person or an object. But you already knew that. Everyone knows what love is, but some people don't know how to show it and therefore don't get to feel this emotion as often as they should. Love works like this: everyone has a love tank. Much like a gas tank, our love tank can be full or it can be empty. It can be filled with premium love or it can be filled with regular. What determines whether the love is premium or regular is the matching of the love given with the type of love the receiver prefers. There are five types of love: kind words, quality time, gifts, services and physical touch. Every person prefers one or two of these types of love over the others. When we match our love with what the person wants, we fill up their love tank with premium love. When we give them a type of love they don't particularly care for, we still fill up their love tank, but with regular love. To maximize the feeling of love in yourself and in others, the goal is to match the love you are giving with the love they want. To do this you're going to have to know some more details about the types of love.

Kind words are compliments, words of encouragement and letting the person know that we love them. Kind words are spoken to the person and about the person when they are not around. Words are kind because of both, the words we are using and how we're using them. When we are kind with our words, we speak soothingly and gently; we make requests as opposed to demands.

Quality time is the time spent with the other person. Quality time is not spent watching a movie, but focused on the other person with one hundred percent of our attention. Quality time is spent listening, making eye contact, reading their body language and responding accordingly. Quality time is spent doing an activity the other person enjoys, and doing it with a smile on our face.

Gifts are something the other person needs or wants. A gift can be extravagant and expensive or a gift can be small with a lot of thought. Services are gifts that don't cost money, but do require effort. A service is cleaning the person's car or accompanying them to the doctor. A service is performed to make the other person's life easier.

Physical touch can be a pat on the back or a hug. Physical touch need not be sexual. It can be a touch of the arm to let the other person know everything is going to be okay. Physical touch can be a back or foot rub, or it can be holding hands while going for a walk.

When we match the type of love we give to the type of love the receiver prefers we are maximizing the feelings of love in ourselves and in the other person. When this happens both people are giving off positive energy, thus attracting back double the positive energy. For this reason love is the most powerful emotion.

You now have procedures to trigger the three basic positive emotions at will. In the long term, being in the state of love will provide the greatest benefit. However, in the short term love costs the most. Showing love to someone takes time, energy and money and if done to the extreme can be draining. Happiness and faith on the other hand require much less in the short term, but their benefits in the long term reflect that. To maximize the amount of positive energy you put out, it is best to oscillate between happiness and love while maintaining a strong faith.

Here is a chart that summarizes how to get yourself in a positive state any time you want:

HOW TO TRIGGER POSITIVE EMOTIONS	
Love	Put someone else first with kind words, quality time, gifts, services or physical touch.
Happiness	Engage in activities that are pleasurable, meaningful and flow-inducing.
Faith	Affirm your belief in a higher power. Visualize how you want your life to be.

MEDITATION

Being aware of the law of attraction, it is easy to see the importance emotions play in what happens in our lives. We attract the same frequency of emotion we transmit, so proactive positivity is of upmost importance. Another reason proactive positivity is important is the law of attraction cannot be turned off. Like other universal laws, like the law of gravity, the law of attraction is working twenty four hours a day, seven days a week. The law of attraction is working even in our sleep. With that being said, although we can't control it, there is a way to slow it down.

As mentioned earlier our thoughts influence our emotions, which are then transmitted into the environment. If we're able to stop thinking, or at least slow down our thoughts, we would be able to have control over how much emotion we transmit. This is particularly useful in times when we are in a pervasive negative mood we can't get out of. The key to this kind of mind control is meditation.

Meditation is the act of focusing our attention on one simple stimulus, for example our breathing, and allowing our minds to enter a state of stillness. This state of stillness clears our thoughts, and in turn clears our emotion or mood which means we are not transmitting as much energy. By meditating we are not stopping the law of attraction, we are just not putting any new energy into the environment. During our meditation our physical bodies are calm and relaxed and we are not performing any action of consequence. Although we're not putting out any energy, energy is still being attracted to us. This leaves us with an excess of energy that can be transformed into whatever we choose. We accumulate energy during our meditation which then has the potential to be focused and released into the environment. Meditation is our tool to slow down the law of attraction just enough so we can transmit the thoughts and emotions we want once our mind is clear.

To practice meditation you must focus on a simple stimulus, such as breathing or a mantra, for long enough to clear your mind and enter into a state of relaxation. It sounds easy, but is deceptively difficult. Clearing your mind and relaxing takes focused attention. Beginners find it difficult to keep their attention on something long enough to reap the benefits of meditation. It is also difficult to keep the mind from wandering; our memory acts up and gets us thinking about the errands we have to run or the confrontation we had at work. We can facilitate the clearing of our minds by not focusing on our thoughts, but instead focusing on the interval between our thoughts. Our thoughts come to us one after the other, but if we look for the gap between them, and focus on that, we can clear our minds more effectively. A useful technique for finding the interval, or gap, is witnessing our thoughts. When a thought enters our mind we don't have to indulge it and analyze it, we can simply acknowledge the thought and let it pass out of our awareness. Once the thought is gone, identifying the interval between our thoughts will be much easier.

Another barrier to meditation is the environment. There are cars driving by, faucets dripping and people talking, which all distract from the task at hand. Meditation can also be stifled by our own expectation of what's going to happen. By anticipating the outcome of our meditation, we stir up anxiety within us, which distracts us. When meditating, it is important to suspend all expectation. If you enter into a state of clear headedness and relaxation, great. If not, it's no big deal. Meditation is a process that you will get better at over time. At first you may only be able to meditate for five or ten minutes, but in time that will grow to twenty minutes, then thirty minutes and so on. Some people are able to meditate for hours. It's all about how much practice you put into it. The good news is that over time it gets easier to initiate and to keep a meditation going. This is particularly true when you meditate in the same place over and over again. Your brain will become accustomed to this space and will prepare itself to meditate just by sitting in the same spot. It will also be quicker and easier to enter a deep meditative state.

The following walk-through will aid you in your practice. Don't refer to this process while meditating, that will only distract you. Instead try to learn it and carry through the process without the aid of the book. Here is a summary of the process to help you remember it:

MEDITATION WALK-THROUGH

Diaphragmatic Breathing	Deep breathing that pushes out your stomach.
Ocean Visualization	Picture an ocean with distractions being carried away by waves.
Systematic Relaxation	Relax each body part by focusing on it.
Energy Visualization	Picture energy filling your body, then filling the world.

Meditation begins with choosing a place to sit. Do not sit in a chair that is too comfortable or you might fall asleep. Sit with good posture and rest your hands on your thighs, or let them dangle on your sides. Begin by breathing deep into your diaphragm. Most of the time we breathe very shallow breaths where only our chest puffs out, then we exhale. Dia-phragmatic breathing is when your stom-ach pushes out and then retracts upon exhaling. While breathing, focus on the sensation of the breath entering your mouth and nose, specifically the sensations on your nostrils and inside your mouth. Focus on your stomach being pushed out and coming back in with every breath.

As you begin to focus on these simple sensations and relax, background noise will become more apparent and distracting. You may also notice your mind drifting. At this time close your eyes and picture yourself in first person, sitting on a lifeguard chair looking out onto an ocean. The water is calm, except for a few small waves that pass by periodically. On these waves, picture your thoughts being carried away. Whatever distracting thought enters your mind, imagine it being carried away on a wave. If you hear a distracting sound, visualize that sound as a wave and watch as it is carried out of your line of view. When these thoughts and noises enter your visualization do not interpret them or give them any thought. Simply let them enter your consciousness and leave your consciousness. Do not think of them as distractions, think of them as something that just is, and continue with your meditation.

After some time, the ocean you are visualizing will become calm and still; all the distractions will have been carried out by the waves. When this happens it is now time to begin a process called systematic relaxation. Start by relaxing your whole body by focusing your attention on one body part at a time. First begin with your toes. Focus on your toes and how they feel. Then move to your feet and ankles. Once everything below your ankles is relaxed, move onto your calves, then your knees, then your thighs and so on until you have relaxed every part of your body up to your crown. When you focus on a body part you may feel a slight tingling sensation; that is the muscles loosening up and relaxing. Relaxing your body should take a sizable portion of time. Do not move onto the next step until you are sure that every body part is relaxed. Take your time and if you doubt that one of your limbs is not as relaxed as it could be, focus on it again and relax it.

When your body is completely relaxed it is time to perform another visualization. This time visualize a bright beam of light or energy coming down on your head from above. Picture this beam entering your body through your crown and filling every relaxed body part from your head to your neck to your shoulders and arms all the way down to your feet. Then imagine the energy exiting your body through your toes. Take some time to feel and enjoy the sensation that comes from this visualization. Feel the energy going through you and filling your body, then begin to visualize the energy expanding inside you. Picture the energy expanding past your skin and creating a bubble around you. Envision yourself inside this energy bubble that continues to expand, filling the room you are in, then filling the home or building. Keep this visualization going until the energy emanating from you has filled your street, your community, your country and eventually the world.

Once you reach this stage of the meditation you can choose to continue and enter deeper states, or you can stop and return to the real world feeling more relaxed and energized. I won't get into the deeper states of meditation partly because once you are at this point you won't need any guidance, and partly because words can't describe how the deeper states feel.

If these meditation techniques are not for you, feel free to create your own. As long as your techniques incorporate the key components of the walk-through mentioned above, anything will work. Simply witnessing your thoughts, emotions and tensions in the body, without getting involved, will lead to a relaxed meditative state. Witnessing can be a powerful meditative technique. When you're on the go, you can witness yourself walking, eating, speaking, listening, and as long as you don't indulge the thoughts that pop into your head, you will enter a mild meditative state. In essence, meditation begins when your mental activity ceases and you are simply in a state of being. So as long as you're not thinking and just being, you're meditating.

When you return to the real world after a meditation, your mind will be stilled and you will be energized because during the meditation you attracted and accumulated energy. With this storehouse of energy, it is important not to waste it on trivial or negative matters. Using the next technique I am going to mention is ideal, but partaking in any kind of positive activity or thought after a meditation will suffice.

PRAYER

Energy plays a large part in our lives, and knowing how to control it and work with it is crucial. We learned that meditation can slow down the law of attraction by controlling our thoughts and emotions. Now we are going to learn how to speed up the process, but first let's examine the concept of energy more closely. Energy, as we've discussed, is the life force behind everything in the universe. Our environment, including ourselves, is made up of energy. We know this because scientists, specifically quantum physicists, have told us so through their research. On the other hand another group of people, theologians, have told us that God has created the universe and is flowing through all forms, including us. Traditionally, science and religion have been at odds with one another, but in more recent times the bridge has been reconciling. The following chart shows how this is so:

COMPARISON OF ENERGY AND GOD

Physicists' Description of Energy	Theologians' Description of God
Can never be created or destroyed.	Can never be created or destroyed.
Always is and has been everything that ever existed.	Always is and has been everything that ever existed.
Moves into and out of forms.	Moves into and out of forms.

As you can see from the chart, the descriptions of energy and God by physicists and theologians are interchangeable. God and energy have the same characteristics; the only difference is the terminology. This is why bad things happen to good people and good things happen to bad people. God is not a person in the sky with unlimited power, but rather a force or energy. God doesn't decide who's fortunate and who's not based on morality, God is indifferent. God – or energy - flows to those people and situations where it is provoked. For example, if you're a good person who follows a religion to the tee out of fear, you will transmit that emotion of fear and attract back to you people, events and circumstances on the same frequency. Even though you are practicing the word of God, which can include positive acts such as helping others, giving to charity etc. You are doing so out of fear, thus you are transmitting that negative emotion with every positive act you perform. On the other hand, say you are a person who has lived a life of vice and has harmed people in the past, but now you are ready to turn your life around. Although while committing your wrongful deeds you have transmitted and therefore will attract negative energy to you, the positive energy you transmit while changing your ways will beget more positive energy. God is not a third party that rewards and punishes behavior; God is a force that operates based on the law of attraction.

Knowing that God and energy are really the same thing, we can now speak about how to accelerate the law of attraction. As mentioned earlier, meditation is the technique used to slow down the law of attraction. Prayer is the technique used to accelerate it. When we pray to God, and genuinely believe our prayer is being heard, we are thinking about what we want and feeling a sense of hope that no matter how big or unrealistic our desire is, it is attainable through the power of God.

Some people are skeptical about the efficacy of prayer. Although research is minimal, studies have confirmed that prayer can be effective in treating illness. In a study that involved ill patients, one group of patients were prayed for, while a control group of patients were not. The group that was prayed for showed an increase in overall well-being greater than that of the control group, thus proving that prayer can be an effective means of affecting the world.

While we pray, we emit more emotion, thus we emit more energy. The energy being attracted to us however remains the same – the law of attraction is consistent and cannot be controlled by us. What we can control is the amount and intensity of emotion we transmit – which is increased through prayer. The reason prayer intensifies our emotion is that when we pray we think about what we want with the intention of summoning God to deliver it to us. This specific intention or thought that God will respond to our prayer creates a sense of faith that is stronger than when we just simply think about what we want. That being said, it is important not to think about anything negative while praying. Since our power to transmit is increased, thinking and feeling negatively will result in an increase of negative emotion being transmitted. If you are praying to God to alleviate a negative situation such as an illness or a difficult circumstance, spend as little time as possible ruminating over the negative aspects and focus on praying for solutions.

Something to keep in mind about prayer is that it's not simply asking God for what you want; that's only part of it. The second and most important part of prayer is having faith and believing that God will come through with what you ask for. In the chapter on proactive positivity we went over what it takes to enter into a state of faith – visualizing what you want and affirming your belief in a higher power. In prayer, affirming your belief is of upmost importance. If you pray and have doubts about the existence of God or in the ability of God to manifest what you are asking for, you will diminish the effectiveness of your prayer. An effective prayer is all about how much faith you can stir up inside of you. Another corollary of praying is that there is strength in numbers. When you pray by yourself you are upping the amount and intensity of emotion you are transmitting. When you pray with others you are increasing that amount relative to the number of people you're praying with; when two or more people come together in faith to pray, the prayer is that much stronger.

Take some time right now to say a prayer. If you've never prayed before or if it's been a while, start by affirming your belief in God, then go ahead and say anything positive that comes to mind, or if you need it, ask for help with a problem you're having. As you begin to pray regularly you will notice God in your life. He will communicate with you through events that seem too extraordinary to be simply a matter of coincidence or chance. God speaks to us in signs and gives us hints as to what the right path is. When you pray you are forming a relationship with God. You tell God what you're thankful for and God will give you more of that. If you ask God for help with a problem, he will give you opportunities to solve that problem. After a while you won't need to formally pray to God. You will be so in touch with God that you will be able to recognize a sign and know instinctively which direction to go. So start right now and say a prayer; soon you will be in constant communication with God.

THE ATTRACTION METHOD

For most people, reading a book of this nature isn't about learning how to work with energy or about the principles that connect us all. Most people read this type of book because they want to learn how to attract a better life. Some people have it easy; they're born into abundant environments and live a life of leisure with minimal hardships. Others have it harder; their experience is one of scarcity and lack, where no matter what action they take, they can never seem to raise their quality of life. The people who struggle through life may wonder if there's something they're missing, something they can learn and apply that will make their lives easier. That something is the attraction method.

Most people read books like this for their practical application. They want a nice car, a big house, a relationship, perfect health and other materialistic things. Others want world peace or to eradicate world hunger or other lofty goals that seem impossible to reach. In this book I've discussed the techniques needed to work with the law of attraction. In this chapter I'm going to put them all together in a cohesive procedure that anyone can follow.

Some people look at those who are successful and wonder how they got there, then after learning the law of attraction it begins to make sense. Anything great that has been achieved has been done so through the use of the law of attraction. Whether the person was aware of it or not, their thoughts attracted the people, events and circumstances that made them successful. When people finally learn the law of attraction, it seems like a whole new world has opened up to them and success is just around the corner. With their new found motivation they begin to think grandiose thoughts about the life they want to have, and aim as high as they can because they now know that anything is possible. They make a list of everything they want to attract; they cut out pictures of cars, houses and people with the bodies they want from magazines and spend their days visualizing their ideal life. In the process, they take themselves out of the present moment. After some time of this positive kick, they get discouraged because they have yet to attract what they wanted, or have attracted an inferior version of what they visualized. For example, instead of attracting brand new relationships, they strengthened their current relationships. Once people realize that the law of attraction doesn't work the way the gurus say it does, they give up on it and move on with their lives. A small percentage of these people become pessimistic, but the majority realize that although they're not living their dream life, the few months of positivity enhanced their life.

My hope is that by reading this book the law of attraction has been demystified. Sure you're not going to be able to attract your dream life in a few months, but over time, through the use of proactive positivity, meditation and prayer, you will radiate positive energy and attract back to you opportunities for getting the things you visualized.

Opportunity is the key word. The law of attraction is not a magical formula to attain anything you want. The universe is not a genie that will grant you everything you desire. The law of attraction brings people who are on the same frequency together. For example, if you're thinking positively and visualizing a brand new car, don't expect the car to suddenly appear in your driveway one morning. The law of attraction doesn't work that way. Instead you may attract a person into your life who gives you an opportunity to make more money to be able to buy that new car. Thinking of ourselves as magnets that can attract whatever we think about is misleading. It can lead people to disbelieve the law of attraction altogether when they discover their magnetism is not as strong as they thought. The law of attraction can attract the opportunities to get what you want in life, but in the end, it depends on your ability to seize the opportunity. The law of attraction may not be able to attract everything you've ever dreamed of, but it is a force to be reckoned with.

In this book we have explored three techniques that can be used to control the energy you transmit and attract to yourself. In this chapter it's time to put proactive positivity, meditation and prayer into action. We will discuss a step by step method you can use to attract the opportunities to acquire what you want in life. The chart on the following page is a summary of the steps involved in this process. (See chart on next page).

The first step, show disinterest, may have thrown you off a bit. This step consists of deciding what you want, then being disinterested in receiving it because you are happy with what you already have. The first part, deciding what you want should be straight forward. Whether you want a better job, better health, world peace or relationships, the fact remains that these are things you don't already have. When you desire something you don't have and have no way of attaining it, it doesn't feel good. Trying to attract something to yourself by simply visualizing it and noticing other people who have what you want, could stir up resentment and jealousy.

The first technique we discussed was proactive positivity. You have to spend life's moments in a positive state. If you want something bad enough and are

THE ATTRACTION METHOD

Show Disinterest	Decide what you want to attract, then show others and yourself that you are disinterested in receiving it because you are happy with what you already have.
Act As If...	Act as if you have already attracted what you desire by developing in yourself the characteristics you would have once you have attracted it.
Take Inspired Action	Meditate to clear your mind, then pray for insight into the next action you should take to get closer to attracting what you want.
Practice Proactive Positivity	Once you have attracted what you want or something that gets you closer to attracting it, resist thinking negatively about what was attracted or the way it was attracted into your life. Be grateful for what you've attracted to yourself.

always noticing that you don't have it, you won't be in a positive mood. Telling yourself that in the future you're going to have what you want plus more, only gives you temporary relief. Eventually it's going to dawn on you that you don't have what you want and your life is not what you want it to be. The key to avoiding these negative thoughts and emotions is to be disinterested in what you want because you are grateful for what you already have. If it's wealth you seek, be disinterested in wealth: who needs a large home? My one bedroom apartment is more than enough. Who needs an expensive car? My ten year old Corolla can get me from point A to point B. Who needs a fit, healthy body? Carrying these extra pounds is a small price to pay for all the delicious foods I get to eat. As you can see, being disinterested is a form of proactive positivity.

Notice that while you're being disinterested, you are not bashing what you want to attract. If you want to attract new

relationships for example, thinking negative thoughts about the type of people
you want to befriend is counterproduc-
tive. Thinking that you don't want to meet
new people because they are below you
in some way is not going to attract them
to you, and worse it makes you feel bitter.
However, thinking that you don't want to
meet new people because you're content
with the people you're already friends
with and grateful for their friendship will
keep you positive, and may even make
you seem more intriguing to others. Being disinterested in the things you want
makes you content with what you already
have and evokes the very strong emotion
of gratitude.

Gratitude is a mixture of happiness
and love, two of the strongest positive
emotions. When you feel gratitude you
are radiating a very strong positive energy
because you love what you already have
and you are happy because there is nothing else you need to do - everything you
love is already yours. The purpose of

showing disinterest is to evoke this strong feeling of gratitude. This step is not easy however, because the feeling of gratitude has to be genuine. You cannot intellectually convince yourself you are grateful, you must actually feel it. You must spend time actually enjoying your life and the things that are already yours. Soon you will learn to love your current life, and showing disinterest for what you want to attract will come naturally. In time you truly won't care about a Mercedes, because you will be perfectly content with your Honda.

The second step in the attraction method is to act as if you have already attracted what it is you desire. This can be achieved at the same time you're showing disinterest for what you want. While you are perfectly happy and showing gratitude for living at home with your parents, you can develop and demonstrate the characteristics you would have once you have moved into your dream home. This step is going to take some visualization.

You have to picture in detail what it will be like to live in your new house. First of all, you are going to have more confidence when you own your mansion, so it's time to start walking with that same strut right now. You need to act like the person who lives in a mansion even though you are living in a tiny bachelor pad. In order to be able to afford your new home, you are going to need a way of making more money. Consider what you could be doing that would allow you to purchase such a beautiful home. Perhaps you can start your own business. Think of what kind of business it is and what kind of characteristics you will need to develop to run that business successfully. You don't need to actually start the business; all you need to do is behave like the person you would imagine owning that type of business.

As you can see, acting as if you have already attracted what you desire is a very creative task. There is no right way of doing it. It all depends on what you honestly believe to be the characteristics you will develop once you have attracted what you desire. The true test of whether or not you are developing these characteristics is what other people are saying about you. When you come into contact with others, they should see you as the type of person who, for example, exercises regularly even though you are out of shape. They should perceive you as the type of person who has many friends even though you are a bit of a loner. You can change people's perceptions by how you behave. You can make people think you are wealthier, healthier and have more relationships by demonstrating the traits associated with each. Once people's perceptions of you change, they will begin to treat you differently and that in turn will reinforce the person you are becoming: the person who has attracted what they desire.

In contrast to showing disinterest to develop genuine gratitude for what you already have, the second step of acting as if you have already attracted what you desire can seem contrived and disingenuous. To a certain extent, it is. Pretending to have the traits of someone who has attracted what they want seems somewhat dishonest. However, you're not going around telling everybody that you have a new car or a new house, you are simply acting like you have these things. If someone asks "have you been working out?" You don't lie and tell them you have; you tell them the truth and let them come to the conclusion that you're the type of person who naturally seems healthy and in shape. When people start to think about you differently, they transmit a different kind of energy in your favor, and this energy helps you attract what you want. Acting as if you have attracted what you don't have yet can be summed up with a simple phrase: fake it to make it.

The third step in the attraction method is to take inspired action. Inspired action refers to an action you have been inspired to take as opposed to an action that seems like the most logical or easiest. For example, if you want to attract more money, the obvious answer is to earn more by putting in longer hours. Although this action will work, it is not an inspired action. If your goal is to attract a brand new luxury car, working more hours to be able to afford the car is not attraction. It is working, saving money and buying a car. An example of an inspired action towards attracting your new car would be to take the first step in starting your own business, or it could be deciding to go get a coffee, where you meet someone who gets you a higher paying job.

To ensure your action is inspired you should start by meditating. When you meditate you clear your mind and are able to operate from a place of stillness. When your mind is cluttered, the action you take will be influenced by all sorts of thoughts and worries. After meditating you will be able to think more clearly about what the right step to take is. After you've meditated and your mind is clear and you are operating from a place of stillness, say a prayer. Pray to God and ask for a way to get you closer to attracting what you want. In your prayer be specific about what you are trying to attract. Tell God that you are not expecting what you want to be given to you, but that you are going to take an action and you would like it to be inspired by God.

Meditating and praying once will probably not be sufficient to conceive of an inspired action to take. However, over time, by repeating this process an idea for inspired action will present itself. When that idea presents itself, don't hesitate. Even if the idea doesn't seem like something that will get you directly to what you want, try it anyway. For example, if you want to attract a new relationship into your life, and after meditation and prayer the best idea for inspired action is to go out to get the newspaper to look for a better job, do it. Perhaps on your way to getting the paper you meet someone, or perhaps you meet someone at the job interview. Take the inspired action when the time seems right. Look for opportunities that God is sending your way. You will know when an opportunity is sent by God because it will be the perfect opportunity to seize. It will be a no-brainer.

One thing to keep in mind with all these steps is that they are not a one-time thing. To attract what you want most likely won't happen with one inspired action, there will be many actions that you need to go through in order to attract what you want. While thinking of these inspired actions and taking them, you must consistently perform the first two steps of showing disinterest and being grateful for what you already have, and acting as if you have already attracted what you want. Once you have taken your inspired action and are successful in attracting what you want, you can stop the first three steps and move onto the final step in the attraction method.

Practicing proactive positivity after your inspired action can take on two forms. First, if your inspired action fails to attract what you desire, you will most likely feel negative about the whole process. In the second scenario, if your inspired action succeeds and you attract what you want, you may still feel negatively if you did not attract exactly what you wanted, or if the manner in which it was attracted was not what you had in mind. First let's examine the scenario where your inspired action fails to attract the thing you want.

There can be many reasons why your inspired action did not attract what you want, but if your action is truly inspired, perhaps it wasn't meant to attract the thing you want just yet. An inspired action can be one of many actions needed to attract what you want. Negative emotions that arise from a perceived failure to attract what you want should be resisted completely. In the worst case scenario, the inspired action was one of many required inspired actions, and the negativity you feel will interfere with the law of attraction bringing you what you've been trying to attract. Practicing proactive positivity is all about using your will power to choose the thoughts that are going to keep you positive. When an inspired action fails, tell yourself that it was one of many inspired actions that will be necessary to attract what you want.

Occasionally when an inspired action fails it may not be that it is one of many inspired actions, but rather the action was not inspired at all. Make sure that before you take an action – especially if the action requires a great deal of effort, time or money – you meditate and pray on it first. Take your time when trying to attract something to yourself. Meditating and praying will ensure that you are following the right path to attracting what you want.

The second scenario where you may need to practice proactive positivity is if the inspired action succeeds at attracting something inferior to what you wanted, or in a manner different from what you visualized. We don't usually attract exactly what we envisioned in exactly the manner we had planned. Every day we project many emotions into the environment, some negative, some positive. This mixture of emotion and thought comes back to us in the proportions it was sent out. It's not likely that we will attract exactly what we want in the exact manner we visualized because as we transmit positive emotions, we also transmit thoughts and feelings of doubt about our ability to attract them. We have to come to terms with what we've attracted into our lives. We have to understand that we did not attract exactly what we wanted in the manner in which we wanted it, not because the law of attraction doesn't work for us, but because we sent out mixed emotions and attracted back mixed results. If you have successfully attracted something to yourself and are still feeling negatively, it's important to resist these negative thoughts and feelings and be happy and grateful with what you have been given.

Applying this method will greatly increase your chances of using the law of attraction to your advantage successfully. More importantly, using this method and the techniques involved will improve your quality of life. As you reach the end of this book, it should become clear to you that you now have the tools to change your life dramatically. By reading this book you have become enlightened. However, as I will explain in the following chapter, en-lightenment doesn't end with a book; it's an ongoing process.

ENLIGHTENED

In the process of writing this book, I have come to the realization that enlightenment is elusive. After filling these pages with ideas and concepts explaining what enlightenment is and how to be enlightened, I realize that enlightenment is not a final destination; it is not a place that once reached, allows one to rest comfortably knowing that he or she knows all there is to know about the mysteries of the universe. In contrast, enlightenment is the beginning of a journey.

Reading a book is one thing, applying what you've learned is another. The techniques I present in this book are only useful if you put in the effort and practice them in your daily life. Proactive positivity will make a difference in your life only if you are able use it when times are difficult. It's easy to be positive when things are going your way, but it's a totally different story when times are challenging. When all you want to do is react to your life circumstances, complain and be negative, that's the time to practice proactive positivity. You're also going to have to take time out of your day to meditate and pray. Even if these techniques are foreign to you, you have to try them out. What you have been doing thus far has gotten you to the point you're at now. If you're serious about turning your life around, you're going to have to try new things. Meditation and prayer are two of those things.

If going through life were like going through a dark cave with writing on the walls, what I have done in this book is analogous to flashing a lantern and giving you a glimpse of the wisdom written on those walls. But it's time for you to take the lantern and explore for yourself. If this is your first self-improvement book, your journey truly is just beginning. If you are well-versed in self-improvement literature, this book is surely a great milestone in your journey as it sums up everything you already knew, and hopefully has taught you something new. My hope now is that you will be able to use this knowledge to live your life to its fullest potential. Good luck going forward.

Made in the USA
Charleston, SC
12 May 2012